THERE IS
RESCUE POWER
IN YOUR TONGUE

THERE IS RESCUE POWER IN YOUR TONGUE

Kingsley Nwokoma

XULON PRESS

Xulon Press
2301 Lucien Way #415
Maitland, FL 32751
407.339.4217
www.xulonpress.com

© 2020 by Kingsley Nwokoma

All rights reserved solely by the author. The author guarantees all contents are original and do not infringe upon the legal rights of any other person or work. No part of this book may be reproduced in any form without the permission of the author. The views expressed in this book are not necessarily those of the publisher.

Unless otherwise indicated, Scripture quotations taken from the King James Version (KJV) – *public domain*.

Printed in the United States of America.

ISBN-13: 978-1-6305-0799-2

TABLE OF CONTENTS

INTRODUCTION ix

1. **WORDS**................................1
2. **CREATIVE POWER IN YOU** 7
3. **WATCH YOUR WORDS** 11
4. **THE POWER OF THE TONGUE** 15
5. **NEGATIVE CONFESSION** 21
6. **BELIEVING AND SPEAKING** 25

BELIEVING 29

INTRODUCTION

"And God said, let there be light; and there was light" (Gen. 1:3).

Words have power. With the words "And God said," God created the world.

These words God spoke came into being. Everything God spoke came into being, and everything He created came into being as a result of His words, which are filled with authority and power.

John 5:26 (NLT) says, "The Father has life in Himself, and He has granted that same life-giving power to His son." Receiving Jesus Christ into your life gives you His power. Choosing to receive Jesus Christ as your Lord and Savior is the most important decision you will ever make, for it is the entrance of this power into your life.

God's Word promises, "If thou shalt confess with thy mouth the Lord Jesus, and shalt believe in thine heart that God has raised Him from the dead, thou shalt be saved. For with the heart, man believeth unto righteousness; and with the mouth confession is made unto salvation" (Rom. 10:9-10).

If you would like to receive Christ, pray out loud, "Jesus, I confess that You are my Lord and Savior. I believe in my heart that God raised You from the dead. By trust and confidence in Your Word, I receive salvation now. Thank You for saving me."

The very moment you commit your life to Jesus Christ, the truth of His Word instantly comes to pass in your spirit. You have been given authority because of Jesus' death, burial, and resurrection. As a born-again child of God, you now have authority, creative authority.

As a result of the authority you have in Jesus Christ, God wants you to overcome the devil and his works with the spoken words of God. Through the words you are speaking, you can change the course of your life. If you need a change from poverty to prosperity, from sickness to health, take a critical look at what you have been speaking and ask the Holy Spirit, the helper, to help you

INTRODUCTION

speak only in accordance with God's words about you. God's Word declares that you were healed by the stripes that were laid on Jesus Christ (1 Pet. 2:24). His word also tells us that God will supply all our needs according to His riches in glory by Christ Jesus (Phil. 4:19).

1. WORDS

God's promises are conceived in your heart, then formed by your tongue and spoken out of your own mouth; they then become a spiritual force releasing the power of God within you.

This is why Paul declared in Philippians 4:13, "I can do all things through Christ which strengthens me." Those who say they can and those who say they can't are both right in their own ways. Words are the most powerful force in the universe.

> James 3:4-5 (MSG) says, "A small rudder on a huge ship in the hands of a skilled captain sets a course in the face of the strongest winds. A word out of your mouth may seem of no account but it can accomplish nearly anything or destroy it. It only takes a spark, to set off a forest on fire."

God has done so much for us, but it's now our responsibility to keep ourselves in His blessings. Just as God told the children of Israel in the wilderness, He is saying to you today, "I have set before you life and death, blessing and cursing" (Deut. 30:19). Through your words, you can choose what you want your life to be. Your mouth is the key that will unlock the blessing of God in your life.

The words you speak will either give you victory over the challenges of life or put you in bondage. Believers have been taken captive by their own words; they have set themselves in a position where they cannot receive from God. They have used their tongue to form the very words that destroy them. In John 1:1, we read, "In the beginning was the Word and the Word was with God and the Word was God." Jesus is the Word of God. Speaking the Word of Word will give you victory over every situation.

With your mouth, you can open the doors of life and allow blessing into your life, and with the same mouth, you can introduce death and curses as well. "For he that will love life and see good days, let him refrain his tongue from evil and his lips that they speak no guile" (1 Pet. 3:10-11). Though your tongue is small, it controls everything in your life; with it, you can chart your course unto a victorious life.

Even prayer produces after its kind. In Mark 11:24, Jesus said, "What things so ever you desire when you pray, believe that you receive them, and you shall have them." This is a spiritual law. God's Word is a spiritual law, yet it functions as a natural law. We have learned to work with natural laws. In dealing with the natural law that governs electricity, we have learned that if we obey and enforce that law, electricity will work for us. But if we continually violate the law which governs electricity, we will get into trouble. As long as we enforce the law that governs electrical forces, it will produce energy to give us light, heat our homes, cook meals, and yet produce no harm to us.

However, if the law that governs electricity is not strictly enforced, this same force can burn, kill, and destroy. Therefore, it is very useful and safe to understand and apply the law that controls electricity.

Similarly, the words that come out of your mouth will work for you to give you victory in life, if you can control those words and bring them into obedience to spiritual law, which is the Word of God. Words governed by the Word of God become spiritual forces that work for you, yet idle words work against you.

The Word of God controls the Spirit world, while man speaking God's Word controls the natural world. The spoken Word of God has creative power ability. "Thou shall decree a thing, and it shall be established unto thee; and the light shall shine upon your ways (Job 22:28)."

You should choose the words of your prayers carefully and speak them accurately. Don't pray defeat. In Mark 11:24, the Word of God says, "What things so ever you desire when you pray, believe you receive." Defeat is not what you desire, so don't pray, say, or expect it.

The wrong choices of words can cause your prayers to work against you. Have you ever used any of these phrases: "Lord, this sickness is killing me," or "Lord, I am so poor"? Don't pray the problem; instead, pray the answer. Mark 11:24 tells us to pray the things we desire, and it is the answer that we desire.

Don't use your words to release faith in the enemy's ability. When you declare what the devil is doing, you have denied the Word of God and made this declaration because of lack of knowledge. Lack of knowledge of God's Word has caused men to be destroyed. In Hosea 4:6, God said, "My people are destroyed for lack of knowledge."

2. CREATIVE POWER IN YOU

Man was created in the image of God and according to the nature of God (Gen. 1:26-27). During creation, creative power flowed from the mouth of God, as we see in Genesis 1:3. "God said, 'Let there be light,' and there was light." According to the Scriptures and the Word of Jesus Christ, you have this same ability residing on the inside of you, if you only believe.

In Mark 16:17-18, Jesus said, "These signs shall follow them that believe; in my Name shall they cast out devils; they shall speak with new tongues; they shall lay hands on the sick and they shall recover." The creative power of God is residing within believers.

Then in Genesis 3:4, there came that snake in the Garden of Eden. The snake said to Eve, "You will not surely die if you eat of that fruit. God knows you will be like Him if you eat of that fruit; you will be wise like God."

Eve ate of the forbidden fruit, and she then talked Adam into doing the same. When Adam ate of the fruit, he turned his power and authority over to the enemy. As a result, Satan became the god of this world. "In whom god of this world hath blinded the minds of them that which believe not, lest the light of the glorious Gospel of Christ who is the image of God, should shine unto them" (2 Cor. 4:4). But Jesus Christ came and got that power back for us. Jesus, who is God's Word, came and took flesh upon Himself.

Jesus was born of a virgin, and this happened through the same way that God created the universe—God said it. The word of God caused a virgin to conceive, bypassing natural occurrence, and bear a child.

God found a woman who agreed with His word that this could be done. In Luke 1:34, we read, "Then said Mary unto the Angel, how shall this be, seeing I know not a man?" Mary didn't doubt this virgin birth could be done; she simply asked, "How?" The answer was, "The Holy Ghost shall come upon you and the power of the Most High shall overshadow thee" (Luke 1:35). In verse 38, Mary said, "Be it done unto me according to thy Word."

Just like God did with Mary, when His word is planted in your spirit, He causes you to become a new creation, for the word of God has declared it.

THE WORD OF GOD MADE FLESH

> John 1:14 says, "And the Word was made flesh and dwelt among us."

In the beginning, the Word was God. This Word came unto Mary, and in Luke 1:38, Mary said, "I receive it, be it done unto me according to Your Word." She first received the Word into her spirit, then it manifested in her physical body. Jesus is the Word of God that came to Mary.

The work of Satan that had been done in Adam was destroying God's creation and His ability to work through man. However, God's Son, Jesus, born through Mary, took back the authority and returned it to man—that is, the believer.

In Matthew 28:18, Jesus stated, "All power is given unto me in Heaven and in earth." He then turned to the believer and said, "These signs shall follow them that believe; in my Name shall they cast out devils; they shall speak with new tongues; they shall lay hands on the sick and they shall recover" (Mark 16:17-8).

Even today, Jesus is saying to anyone who has received Him as Lord and personal Savior; "In my Name, go and cast out demons, speak with new tongues, lay hands on the sick and they will recover."

The enemy knows there is power in your words and is desperately trying to get you to confess doubt, fear, and unbelief, so take hold of the words of Jesus.

3. WATCH YOUR WORDS

When you start speaking fear, lack, and sickness, such as statements like, "I am so poor," or "I am so sick," you start releasing Satan's ability to destroy your faith.

Before you ever make a confession of what comes into your head, ask yourself, "Is this in line with the Word of God? What is its source?" If your thoughts don't agree with the Word of God, then the devil has spoken it to you, and mustn't ever quote it. If you do, you will activate his deception.

The devil even spoke through Peter, a servant and apostle of Jesus Christ. In Matthew 16:15, Jesus Christ said unto His disciples, "'But whom say ye that I am?' And Simon Peter answered, 'Thou are the Christ, the Son of the living God.' And Jesus said unto him, 'Bless are thou

Simon Barijona. For flesh and blood have not revealed it unto you, but my Father which is in Heaven.'"

In this passage, Jesus is saying that God gave Peter this revelation of Him. The chapter continues, with Matthew 16:21-23 (AMP):

> From that time forth, began Jesus to show unto His disciples how that He must go into Jerusalem and suffer many things of the elders and chief priest and scribes and be killed and be raised from the dead the third day.
>
> Then Peter took Him and began to rebuke Him, saying, "Be it far from the Lord, this shall not be unto the thee." But Jesus turned and said to Peter, "Get thee behind me, Satan, you are a stumbling block to me; for you are not settling your mind on things of God, but on the things of men."

The same Peter that Jesus had said had a revelation about Him was the same person Jesus turned to and said, "Get behind me, Satan."

The devil can speak through anyone, so you must always bring every thought and word to the obedience of God's Word.

When you say, "The devil is hindering me; the devil won't let me do what I want to do," you have immediately stopped God's ability and have established Satan's word. When you tell people around you what the devil is doing, you have established the words of Satan in your life.

The Word of God says, "In the mouth of two or three witnesses shall every Word be established" (2 Cor. 13:1). Fear activates the devil, but faith brings God on the scene.

AUTHORITY OF WORDS

Jesus never talked any foolishness when He spoke. He always meant wha He said and said what He meant. In Matthew 12:36, Jesus said, "But I say unto you, that every idle word that men shall speak, they shall give account thereof in the day of judgement."

THERE IS RESCUE POWER IN YOUR TONGUE

The word "idle" means non-effective. Jesus was saying that in the day of judgement, you will have to account for every word you spoke that was not working for you. Even if you believe the Bible, if you don't control your tongue, it will cause God's Word to become ineffective in your life.

You need to know what the Word of God says and start saying it accordingly. Watch your words.

4. THE POWER OF THE TONGUE

The tongue can either destroy you or give you victory over every situation. In James 3:10, the Bible says, "Out of the mouth proceeded blessing and cursing. My brethren, these things ought not so to be."

This is not supposed to be so. Jesus stated in Matthew 12:34, "O generation of vipers, how can you being evil, speak good things? For out of the abundance of the heart, the mouth speaketh." In these verses of the Scripture, Jesus teaches us that the mouth speaks out of that which fills the heart.

What you put in abundance into your heart is what you will speak. What is the abundance of your heart? Your heart is programmed by your words. The Scripture says, "So then faith cometh by hearing and hearing by the Word of God" (Rom. 10:17). Similarly, fear comes by hearing what the enemy said, and many believers have been listening to the enemy and have continually confessed the words of their enemy. By doing this, they help to establish the words of their enemy on earth and thereby are held back or in bondage by their words.

The devil's words are designed to work against you. Don't use his words; stop calling yourself a liar, a thief, or an unworthy sinner. These words work against you by creating a distorted, unworthy, self-destructive image on the inside of you—in your spirit—with words authored by the enemy of your soul.

In Matthew 12:35, Jesus reveals, "A good man out of the good treasure of the heart bringeth forth good things." He said that man brings forth God's favor and protection not out of his head or intellect but out of his heart.

Matthew 15:11 says, "Not that which goeth into the mouth defileth a man, but that which cometh out of the mouth, this defileth a man." Both blessing and cursing of life come out of the heart and are released through the mouth.

THE POWER OF THE TONGUE

"But those things which proceed out of the mouth come forth from the heart; and they defile the man. For out of the heart proceed evil thoughts, murders, adulteries, fornications, thefts, false witnesses, blasphemies" (Matt. 15:18-19).

When a believer has an abundance of God's Word in his heart and speaks those words forth in faith, he speaks words of the Spirit. These words will dominate the physical and natural world. The believer breathes Spirit life into God's Word, and it becomes a living substance working for him, just as it worked for our Lord and Savior Jesus Christ when He cursed the fig tree and it dried up from the roots.

> "And Jesus answered and said unto it, no man eat fruit of thee hereafter forever. And His disciples heard it" (Mark 11:14).

"And in the morning as they passed by, they saw the fig tree dried up from the roots. And Peter calling to remembrance saith unto the Master, behold, the fig tree which thou cursed is withered away. And Jesus answering saith unto them, have faith in God" (Mark 11:22).

In John 6:63, Jesus said, "The Words that I speak unto you, they are spirit and they are life." The Words Jesus refers to here are the words of God, which He received into His Spirit. With these words abundantly in His heart, Jesus released faith in word form through His mouth, and His words penetrated the spirit of man. Their spirits heard Him, and they acted from their spirits with spirit words.

The words Jesus spoke were truly spirit words, full of life. In Mark 5:41, Jesus said, "Damsel, I say unto thee, arise," and in John 11:43, He said, "Lazarus, come forth."

Just as Jesus showed us through His words, death and life are in the power of the tongue. Therefore, the words of your mouth and the meditation of your heart need to be acceptable in the sight of the Lord. "Don't let corrupt communication proceed out your mouth, but that which is good to the use of edifying that it may minister grace to the hearers" (Eph. 4:29).

Many verses in the Bible tell us about the power and consequences of our words.

Proverbs 18:20 (AMP) says, "A man's moral self shall be filled with the fruit of his mouth and with consequences of his words, he must be satisfied."

Proverbs 18:21 (AMP) says, "Death and life are in the power of the tongue, and they that love it shall eat the fruit of it."

Proverbs 13:3 (AMP) says, "He who guards his mouth keeps his life."

5. NEGATIVE CONFESSION

Maurice Horn said, "Some people confess a sin a thousand times. I tell them to confess it once, then thank God a thousand times for forgiving them."

Satan knows that God has given us authority in the earth, and we express and use this authority through our words. Therefore, Satan is attacking us, even through our words. He wants to destroy our understanding of the power and value of our words. This power and value is something God has given us, for He wants us to live a blessed life.

As a result of Satan's words, we stop believing that anything we say will come to pass or have any consequences. Satan often convinces us that our words are not spirit nor life, that words are only empty speech.

Jesus said His words are spirit and full of abundant life, with spiritual power to overcome any natural challenge.

THERE IS RESCUE POWER IN YOUR TONGUE

In John 6:63, He stated, "It is the Spirit that quickened; the flesh profiteth nothing; the Words that I speak unto you, they are Spirit, and they are life."

When you speak life-giving words of faith, you release unlimited power. No matter what you are going through, you can access the life-altering power of the utterance of God's Word.

We must know the power of our own words upon our spirit, for there is power in confession of the Word of God. If I confess that I am sick, my spirit revolts against that negative confession, but it is conquered by my words. Then I become spiritually and mentally what I confess.

However, if I confess that I can do all things in Christ, He becomes the level of my confession. When I believe and confess that I can do all things in Him, He becomes the strength of my life. Therefore, my confession invites God to do all that He wishes for me to do. My faith rises to the level of my confession, and God's ability in me rises to bring the manifestation of my confession.

NEGATIVE CONFESSION

We have certain words in our vocabularies that should be forgotten and never permitted on our lips. If we refuse to speak them after some time, those Satanic thoughts will die. For example, we should stop using the word "fear" until fear dies and courage grows abundantly in its place. Likewise, we should have no room for such words as "scandal," "jealousy," "unbelief," "hatred," "bitterness," or "doubt," or expression like, "I am doubting Thomas." By using such words, we are telling God that we do not have faith in Him. We ought to become so ashamed of such words that we will never permit them to be spoken in our presence.

We also have words that we speak only in the privacy of our own inner lives, but these should never be spoken either, not even privately. Let us find words of love, health, and victory to take the place of the negative words in our lives.

Don't allow your feelings to control your words, for your feelings change like the weather. Instead, allow the Word of God to control your words, as you live by faith.

6. BELIEVING AND SPEAKING

Jesus illustrated the power of words spoken in faith through the story of the fig tree. In Mark 11:11-14, the disciples heard Jesus speaking to the tree, which had no ears or mouth, nor any way of communication.

After Jesus cursed the fig tree, He didn't go back to check on the tree every minute to see if the words He had spoken worked. He knew the tree was as good as gone, for He believed everything He said would come to pass.

Jesus Christ cursed the fig tree because it was barren, for fig trees are for making figs. We plant apple trees because we want apples, peach trees because we want peaches. We might as well ask, what good is an apple tree that doesn't produce apples? You might as well cut it down or curse it, just as Jesus did the fig tree in Mark 11:12-14.

Jesus knew the fig tree was barren because the leaves and fruits of fig trees typically appear at about the same time. To see a fig tree covered with leaves but no fruits meant that it was barren.

When Jesus and His disciples passed by the fig tree and saw what had happened to it, Peter was astonished. "And Peter calling to remembrance saith unto Him, Master, behold the fig tree which thou cursed is withered away. And Jesus answering, saith unto them, Have faith in God" (Mark 11:21-22).

The wind also obeyed the voice of Jesus. Mark 4:39 says, "Jesus spoke to the wind and said unto the sea; peace be still, and the wind ceased and there was a great calm."

Whenever you are praying and declaring the Word of God with your mouth, you need to have faith in Him to perform His Word.

If you are having hard time believing the word you are praying, just keep confessing it until it becomes more real to you than any problem you are facing. Faith comes by hearing, and hearing by the Word of God. So keep hearing the truth, and soon, faith will rise and the Word of God will be established in your heart.

We have to believe that after we have spoken God's Word over our situation, we can walk away and rest knowing that the word we spoke carried the power of God and what we said must come to pass.

Satan's biggest deception is making you believe that your words have no power or value. He does not want you to believe anything you say, especially when you are speaking God's words over a situation. I want you to know that unlimited power is released when you speak life-giving words of faith. No matter what you are going through, uttering God's Word releases life-altering power. Speaking the Word with confidence will enable you fulfil God's plan and purpose for your life.

Irrespective of your situation, today's mountain is tomorrow's testimony. It doesn't matter how big the mountain is or how long it has been there; what matters is what Jesus said about the mountain. You can be victorious over the mountains of life, if you will only speak to them (Mark 11:23).

BELIEVING

Believing is an action word, and faith is the result of a person having acted on or believing in the Word of God. Proverbs 3:5 tells us that believing is "to trust in and rely confidently on the Lord with all your heart and do not trust on your own insight or understanding."

The key to belief is found in John 6:47, in which Jesus said, "He who believes in me has everlasting life."

In the mind of God, believing is possessing whatever you desire in His will, which is His Word, when you pray (Mark 11:24). Believing is an act of the will, a choice and a decision.

In the kingdom of God, there is no such thing as possession without speaking it forth. Believing and speaking means holding fast your words and confessions and speaking what God has said until the thing that you have desired in your heart, which was promised in the Word of God, is fully manifested.